DATE DUE

SP 2 3			
JE 16 76			

Argentina

Argentina is a "new" nation. In the 1820s, it was emerging from 200 years of Spanish rule: an undeveloped, underpopulated country – one of the world's empty spaces. Today, it is the second most important country in South America, after Brazil.

This transformation is almost entirely due to utilizing the Pampas. Its products, especially meat and grain, account for 85 percent of Argentina's exports. Large-scale British investment and the arrival of many skilled European immigrants has

also aided development.

In recent years, economic and social progress has been hampered by unstable government, both civil and military, which has led to high unemployment and soaring inflation – reaching 443 percent in the mid-Seventies.

A South American freelance photo-journalist, Alex Huber has traveled throughout Argentina to gather these twenty-six accounts of life in its cities, countryside and industry.

we live in
ARGENTINA

Alex Huber

The Bookwright Press
New York · 1984

Living Here

We live in Argentina

We live in Australia

We live in Britain

We live in China

We live in Denmark

We live in France

We live in Greece

We live in India

We live in Israel

We live in Italy

We live in Japan

We live in Kenya

We live in New Zealand

We live in Spain

We live in West Germany

First published in the United States in 1984 by
The Bookwright Press, 387 Park Avenue South,
New York, NY 10016

First published in Great Britain in 1984 by
Wayland (Publishers) Ltd
49 Lansdowne Place, Hove
East Sussex BN3 1HF, England

© Copyright 1984 Wayland (Publishers) Ltd

ISBN 0–531–03793–2
Library of Congress Catalog Card Number: 84–70775

Printed in Italy by G. Canale & C.S.p.A., Turin

Contents

Maria Sanz, *folk-dancer*   6

José Indelacato, *train engineer*   8

José Snihur, *yerba farmer*   10

Juan Gonzales, *soldier*   12

Juan Roberts, *café owner*   14

Maria Yupanqui, *Diaguita Indian*   16

Julian Garcia, *priest*   18

Santiago Labbe, *gaucho*   20

Emille Macchi, *nuclear power plant worker*   22

Jorge Pittaluga, *polo player*   24

Alberto Casaroli, *national park warden*   26

Oscar Vilora, *truck driver*   28

Rosa Valdes, *frigorifico worker*   30

José Galindez, *local politician*   32

Alejandro Sera, *wine producer*   34

José Balseiro, *museum guide*   36

Isabel Gil, *tango dancer*   38

Ferdinando Martin, *tourist boat skipper*   40

Santiago Lara, *cattle farmer*   42

Luis Manzano, *politician*   44

Ana Solis, *agricultural student*   46

Rumualdo Diaz, *small-farm owner*   48

Juan Alonso, *chocolate maker*   50

Italo Colluccini, *croupier*   52

Silvia Rolandi, *TV broadcaster*   54

Marcelo Roa, *schoolboy*   56

Facts   58

Glossary   59

Index   60

"Our environment has influenced our dancing"

Maria Sanz, 16, lives in the city of Salta, in northwestern Argentina. She started ballet when she was 6, and is now a member of a folk-dancing group. Salta is famous throughout the country for producing good folk dancers.

Our style of folk-dancing stems from the days when a gaucho used to dance with his girlfriend, his *paisana*, to demonstrate his affection and respect for her. When we dance, even during rehearsals, the music makes us all feel very romantic. There are six couples in this group, three of whom are engaged. My dancing partner is also my boyfriend.

Folk-dancing is very demanding. Consequently, most dancers are under 25 and the best ones are in their teens. The older you get, the less energy you have and your dancing loses its vitality and vigor.

The folk-dancing group rehearses during the week and gives performances on weekends.

Dancing is very popular in this area and has a long history. It started with the Incas, and then the Spaniards came and added their music and styles of dancing. The music and dancing today is a mixture of these two cultures. There is an old Indian saying that *La Pacha Mama* (Mother Earth) gave the gift of music to the men of this region. Even today, the best folk-dancers in Argentina come from this part of the country.

Our environment has influenced our music, the style of dancing and the costumes we wear. Salta is surrounded by mountains with fertile, green valleys between them, so we feel that we are safe and protected. This is reflected in our dancing: it's intimate and jolly. Down on the Pampas, the music and dancing is like the

Folk-dancing is physically demanding, so the best performers are under 25 years old.

scenery – rather more ponderous and monotonous than ours.

Our folk-dancing and music is also influenced by the cultures of our neighboring countries. In this part of Argentina, there are many similarities with Bolivian music and dancing; the northeast has Paraguayan influences; and the west, Chilean.

We rehearse three times a week and give performances almost every weekend. We're very selfish performers – our own satisfaction and pleasure comes first, and then our audience's. Folk-dancing is a very emotional experience for us.

"One of the largest networks in the world"

José Indelacato moved from Buenos Aires to Salta fourteen years ago. He has been working on the railroads for the last thirty-four years. Currently, he is the engineer of a freight train on the line between Salta and Socompa, high in the Andes Mountains.

The track between Salta and Socompa, a distance of 600 km (375 miles), is one of the most difficult in the country. There are at least 3,000 bends in it and some very steep inclines. It takes about forty hours to make the trip. There is an amazing piece of engineering at one point: the curved, iron Polvorillas Bridge, 224 meters (735 feet) long and 63 meters (208 feet) high.

The track has a narrow gauge, 1 meter (3.3 feet) wide, which helps the trains negotiate the bends. The diesel locomotive weighs 100 tons and has 1,250 horsepower (that's about twenty times more powerful than an average family car engine). Its air filter has been specially adapted to work at high altitudes. It can pull about 1,000 tons of minerals, such as copper, lead, iron and silver, from the mines in the Argentine part of the Andes.

I used to drive trains across the flat Pampas of Buenos Aires Province. When I was transferred up here, I was immediately enchanted by the magnificent mountain scenery. But when I'm in the cab, I've got to keep my eyes on the track ahead because landslides and rock falls are very common. This line used to be used only during the day for many years, but with improved communications, it's now in use day and night.

They began building this stretch of track at the start of the 1920s, under the supervision of the famous Argentine railroad engineer, Mr Maury. One of his lifelong ambitions was to connect the northwestern part of Argentina with the Chilean port of Antofagasta, on the Pacific Ocean. It took twenty-five years just to build the Argentine part of the line.

There are some 40,250 km (25,000 miles) of railroads in Argentina, one of the largest networks in the world. It was started in the 1870s by foreign companies, mainly British and French, to help them take our cattle to the *frigorificos* on the coast. The system was nationalized in the 1940s. Now we build locomotives and railroad cars under license, and have begun to export them to other countries.

Right from the start, the railroad network has centered on Buenos Aires, the main port of Argentina. Some parts of the country are still poorly served by railroads, and in Patagonia there are virtually no trains. But it is planned to expand the network because trains are the most efficient way of moving people and goods.

José sometimes drives passenger trains. Here he picks up people from mountain villages to take them down to the plains.

The Polvorillas Bridge, an amazing feat of engineering high up in the Andes Mountains. It is 224 m (735 ft) long and 63 m (207 ft) high.

"Yerba is our national drink... it's addictive!"

José Snihur, 60, owns a 35-hectare (87-acre) farm, with 8 hectares (20 acres) of yerba trees. The farm is near Apostoles, in the Province of Misiones, northeastern Argentina. The farm was started by José's father, an immigrant from Armenia.

Yerba grows naturally in Argentina. It is an evergreen tree of the holly family. It was first made into a drink by the Indians, then it became so popular that it's now our national drink.

Yerba is grown mainly in the southern part of Misiones Province and in the northern part of Corrientes Province, in the northeastern part of the country. Apostoles is one of the largest producers, because the tree flourishes in the red soil around here; black soil is no good for

growing yerba. It needs a lot of sun, not too much rain and a low humidity. Yerba's main enemy is the cold. It is harvested twice a year, in May and September, and growers must be careful not to remove too many branches, which would leave the trees exposed to the cold. We don't use any fertilizers. The key to a healthy tree is constant pruning and keeping it free of weeds. If this is done, then it can grow for over a hundred years.

To start a yerba plantation, you need the permission of the organization that controls its production in Argentina. There are thousands of small growers like myself in this region. At the end of the harvest, we take the branches to a mill, where they are dried over wood fires for about twenty hours. The brittle leaves are then shaken off, crushed, packaged and sold. There is only one type of yerba tree, but what the final product tastes like depends on how

About a quarter of José's farm is planted with yerba trees, which are harvested twice a year.

the mill has dried the branches.

Over the last five years, our yerba harvest has fetched good prices. But there have been times, like 1966, when too much was produced and prices fell – so much so that it wasn't worth harvesting. Argentina keeps most of the yerba for itself, only exporting about 2 percent of the annual production.

I get up at 5 a.m. every day and always have a *maté* (a metal pot) of yerba before doing anything. During the harvest, I start work at 5:30 a.m. and finish in the early evening, with a break of three hours at lunch time, the hottest part of the day. This is the first year when we have had to employ other people to help with the harvest. My wife and I used to do it all, picking between 500 and 600 kg (1,100 and 1,320 lb) of branches a day; but at our age we don't work as quickly as we used to.

Traditionally, yerba is drunk with a group of friends. You put the yerba in a *maté* and then pour boiling water over it. You drink it through a *bombilla* (a metal drinking straw). When the *maté* is empty, it's refilled with water and then passed on to someone else. It's usually drunk without sugar. It has a bitter flavor, is good for your digestion and, believe it or not, is very nourishing. It contains caffeine, so it wakes you up, as well. I think it's very addictive!

The harvested yerba leaves are stirred up constantly, allowing air to circulate, so that they do not rot.

"Fourteen months of compulsory military service"

Juan Gonzales is in the middle of his compulsory military service with *Los Granaderos de San Martin* (the Grenadiers of San Martin), a regiment based in Buenos Aires and one of the oldest in the country.

This regiment, together with the one called *Los Patricios* (the Patricians), is the oldest in the country. We used to be the personal guard to General San Martin, the father of our nation, who freed the Argentine people from the Spaniards at the beginning of the last century.

We provide a guard outside the presidential palace, the *Casa Rosada* (the Pink House). When we are standing guard, we wear the same uniform that soldiers did in General San Martin's time. It's very heavy, especially the helmet, and hot – ideal for our winters, but murder during the hot humid summers in Buenos Aires, when many soldiers faint because the weight of the helmet restricts the flow of blood to your head.

When it's your turn to be on guard, you spend a week being on duty from 7:30 a.m. to 7:30 p.m., standing on guard for one and

One of the beautiful squares of the capital, Buenos Aires, where Juan is based.

A parade to mark Army Day, celebrated on May 25 each year.

a half hours and then resting for an hour and a half.

This regiment also provides a guard for the tomb of General San Martin in the cathedral and at the President's official residence at Olivos, about an hour by car from the center of Buenos Aires — or ten minutes by helicopter!

Standing on guard is only part of my army life. This regiment is a real military unit, as well. We have modern uniforms and equipment which we use when we're not on guard duty. Although we are based in the capital, we regularly go on training exercises in the countryside. In this regiment, we do fourteen months of compulsory military service, two more than the normal twelve months in other units, because we get specialized training.

There are 160,000 soldiers in the Argentine Army, 28 percent of whom are career people; the remainder being draftees like myself. There are 55,000 men in the Navy and 29,000 in the Air Force; 50 percent of these are career people.

Argentina produces much of its own military equipment: rifles, machine guns, pistols, small tanks and military trucks for the Army; training planes for the Air Force; and small patrol boats for the Navy. Some of this equipment is exported to other countries in South America, and we are now looking for markets in Africa and parts of Asia.

13

"Patagonia is a cool desert"

Juan Roberts is a descendant of one of the Welsh immigrants who came to Patagonia in 1865. He and his wife run a café in Gaiman. Juan has always been very interested in the history of this region. Agriculture is the main activity but coal, oil and gas are being extracted.

Patagonia was named after *Patagon*, a legendary, extremely tall Indian. The region lies on a plateau sloping from the Andes down to the Atlantic, about 600 meters (2,000 feet) above sea level. The plateau is crossed by broad, steep-sided valleys which were filled with water from melting ice-sheets at the end of the Ice Age. The valleys now have rivers, bordered by wide strips of cultivable soil.

The rest of the land is barren, covered with stones and coarse grass.

Our winters are cold and the summers warm. Because we are in the rain shadow of the Andes, we get little rain – about 230 mm (9 in) a year. So Patagonia can be described as a "cool desert."

I'm a direct descendant of one of the 153 Welsh people who landed in Port Madryn in 1865. They were poor people who were escaping from the crowded mining valleys and from an English Parliament which had banned Welsh from being taught in schools and opposed a Welsh independence movement. They chose Patagonia because it was far away from English people! The Argentine government gave the settlers some land along the River Chubut, 64 km (40 miles) across the desert from Port Madryn.

The immigrants were very friendly with the Indians and opposed the so-called

Juan's café is very busy at weekends, when people come to Gaiman to do their shopping.

14

Patagonia lies on a sloping plateau, which is crossed by broad, steep-sided valleys like this one.

"War of the Desert," during which the Indians were almost exterminated by the Argentine Army from Buenos Aires. My ancestors began farms and were soon growing good-quality wheat. They also started breeding sheep in the sheltered valleys. Patagonia's *estancias* now have the majority of the country's 46 million sheep and help to make Argentina the world's fourth largest wool-producing nation. In the warmer, northern parts of Patagonia, apples, pears and grapes are grown with the help of irrigation projects.

This café was opened by my wife's aunt, who thought that the farmers visiting Gaiman for their shopping would like somewhere to have a drink and a bite to eat. It was a great success and other people soon copied her. We serve tea and homemade biscuits, bread and jam. We're very busy on weekends when whole families come to Gaiman to do their shopping.

In 1981, my wife and I went to Wales for the first time. The countryside was beautiful and everyone was very friendly, but we would never leave here. This is our home. We're Argentine, not Welsh. Many of the people of my generation still speak Welsh, but our grandchildren aren't interested in learning it.

15

"The Sun, the Moon and the Earth are our main gods"

Maria Yupanqui is a Diaguita Indian who lives high up in the Andes Mountains, about 100 km (62 miles) west of Salta. Traditionally farmers, the community which she belongs to now earns money by selling home-woven textiles to tourists.

Diaguita Indians have lived in this region for generations. Life has never been easy for us at this altitude – 3,000 meters (9,800 feet). There is less oxygen up here than at sea level, and the variations in temperature are more extreme. It can get very hot during the day, and yet be very cold at night. Also, the soil is of very poor quality. This area used to be part of the Inca Empire before the Spaniards conquered it in the sixteenth century.

We are mainly a farming community. We grow beans, corn and potatoes on the mountain slopes. To irrigate these crops, we still use the channels built centuries ago by our ancestors. We also breed llamas. The llama is a very useful animal which provides us with wool, meat, and a

Maria selling some clothes she has made to passengers from the "Tren a las Nubes" ("Train to the Clouds").

Indians waiting at the railway station for the arrival of the "Tren a las Nubes".

means of transportation. Animals like sheep and cattle cannot survive at this altitude. In our community, the more llamas you own, the richer you are.

Our life styles have altered a little since tourists started coming here. The looms in our homes used to be used only for weaving clothes for the family, using wool from llamas. Nowadays, many of the clothes are for selling to tourists. We always go down to the station to meet the *Tren a las Nubes* (Train to the Clouds) which stops here to let people stretch their legs. Many tourists travel on it and we sell them things like blankets, socks, scarves and sweaters. The income we get from this trade is used to buy things we cannot produce ourselves — everything from radios to a small truck.

Our homes are houses made with stones, held together with a mixture of straw and clay. We live in small, independent communities. Each community has

its own leader, either a man or a woman, who is usually one of the respected elder members. You can tell to which community someone belongs by the way they dress, the color of their clothes, and the hairstyle of the women.

We consider ourselves Argentines, although we have kept many of our ancestral customs. Religion for us is a mixture of Christianity and our own beliefs. *Inti* (the Sun), *Mama Hilla* (the Moon) and *Pacha Mama* (the Earth) are our main gods. We also have minor gods for thunder, rain and lightning. There are festivals throughout the year which are dedicated to our gods. During them, our community organizes huge parties with music, singing and dancing, and lots of food! The most important festival is the one for *Inti*.

"Catholicism came here with the Spaniards"

Julian Garcia is a Franciscan friar. Born in Spain, he has lived in Argentina for thirty years. He is the administrator of a monastery near Salta and is planning to have a gigantic statue of St Francis of Assisi erected nearby. Julian is holding a model of it in the picture on the left.

This is a Franciscan monastery where people from all over the world come to attend religious meetings or come just for some peace and quiet. I'm responsible for running it.

Our order was founded by St Francis of Assisi and is part of the Catholic Church. We are currently having a statue of St Francis built. It will be completed by 1985, the eight hundredth anniversary of his birth. The statue will be 33 meters (109 feet) high.

Each religious order of the Catholic Church is involved in different aspects of life. Some look after the sick, others run schools, and others deal with prisoners. We are a contemplative and missionary order, which means that we pray a lot and go out to try to convert people to our faith. We have three vows: obedience, chastity and poverty. In religious matters, we follow the orders of the bishop of this diocese, and he deals directly with the Vatican in Rome.

Ninety percent of our population is Catholic. Catholicism came here with the Spaniards about 400 years ago. In those days, priests had to be very brave to go off into unknown areas to convert the

The Franciscan church in Salta, reputed to have the tallest belfry in South America.

The city of Salta, a religious center, with more churches than any other city in Argentina.

Indians, who were often very unfriendly. Some priests never returned.

One of the most famous incidents in the history of the Catholic faith in Argentina is the story about the statue of Christ on the cross in Salta Cathedral. It was being brought here from Spain, via present-day Chile, in the seventeenth century, when the ship carrying it was sunk in a storm at sea. Mysteriously, the statue floated to Callao, near Lima in Peru. From there, it was carried by horse across the Andes to Salta, a distance of about 1,000 km (1,600 miles). There were great celebrations in the city when the statue arrived, after which it was put in the cathedral's cellar.

There was a big earthquake in the area a hundred years later and the worried people of Salta went to the cathedral to pray. There they heard a voice saying that the earthquake would stop only if the statue was put in its proper place in the cathedral. The congregation then went down to the cellar, took the statue out and paraded it around the city before returning it to the cathedral. The earthquake stopped. Now, each year, the statue is taken around the city to commemorate the event.

Salta is still a very religious city. I have been told that it has more churches than any other city in the country.

"Roads and railroads changed our lives"

Santiago Labbe is a gaucho who lives in San Antonio de Areco, Buenos Aires Province. There have been gauchos in this area for generations because of the many *estancias* (large cattle ranches) there. The life of a gaucho has changed a lot since the beginning of the century.

Gauchos are part of this province's history. This was the first area to be settled by the Spanish when they came in the sixteenth century. The Spanish took land away from the native Indians, and gauchos helped them to start farms.

A gaucho is very similar to the North American cowboy. He is a farm-hand who does such things as taking care of the cattle, repairing fences and taming wild horses so that they can be ridden.

Until the turn of the century, the main job of a gaucho was to take the cattle to the markets in Buenos Aires, riding for weeks on end through the *estancias* of the Pampas. But the building of roads and railroads, and the breaking up of many of the large farms, changed his life. Now, we drive motorcycles and tractors instead of riding horses, and need to know how to repair engines and how to vaccinate cattle against disease. We've even got television and radios! Things have certainly changed – probably for the better, though.

One thing that has been lost forever is our independence – the feeling of being free to go where you wanted, when you wanted. In the past, wherever you went,

Even today, gauchos often meet around an asado *(barbecue) after a hard day's work.*

whether it was in the Pampas or in Patagonia, there was always work to be done on the *estancias*, which were much larger then. There were no fences around them, either. It was just like the American Wild West – with Indians, hold ups, and "good guys and bad guys" too!

But some of our customs remain, like trying to tame wild horses. We used to have to do this out of necessity. Now it's a popular sport at rodeos. Around San Antonio de Areco, rodeos are held in the first week of November. It's quite frightening to see the bucking broncos trying to shake off their riders, who hang on in any way they can. In my last rodeo, the horse I was on reared up and fell on its back, trapping me underneath it. That accident crippled my right leg for life.

Despite all the upheavals, the true spirit of gaucho life hasn't altered. To be a gaucho is to belong to a big fraternity where there is a code of honor and friendship. After a hard day's work, gauchos still meet around an open fire, drinking yerba in a *maté* and chatting, waiting for the *asado* (barbecued meat) to cook. And we still express our feelings through music and song. These come deep from the heart and are usually about the love of a woman or a long-lost comrade. They're monotonous and sad, reflecting the landscape around here and how our lives used to be – hard work, with limited prospects.

The gaucho's "home" – the wide-open plains of the Pampas of Buenos Aires Province.

"Enough reserves of uranium for forty years"

Emille Macchi has been working at Atucha I, the first nuclear power station in South America for the last ten years. The power station is near her home in Zarate. She is also taking a part-time computer course at Buenos Aires University.

All nuclear energy matters are controlled by the CNEA (*Comision Nacional de Energia Atomica*/National Commission for Atomic Energy), set up nearly thirty years ago.

There are two nuclear power stations in operation at the moment. Atucha I, where work, is situated 100 km (63 miles) from the capital. It began generating electricity in 1974. Some one and a half million TV sets can be powered by all the electricity it

Emille does not work in a high-risk area, but she has a medical check up every six months.

Another nuclear power plant is being built alongside Atucha I, which will be working in the late 1980s.

produces! The second power station is at Embalse, in Cordoba Province. It was opened in May 1983.

Another power station is being built alongside Atucha I, which should be operational by the end of the 1980s. Another three nuclear power stations should be working by the end of this century.

The heat produced in a nuclear reactor is used to turn water into steam, which turns turbines to generate electricity. Our reactors use uranium for fuel, because we have large natural reserves of it, mainly in Mendoza Province. It has been calculated that we have enough reserves of uranium to last for forty years.

The main aim of the CNEA is to make Argentina totally self-sufficient in nuclear power, so that we don't have to import any technology from other countries. We have been able to process our own uranium into nuclear fuel, called radioactive isotopes, for the last twenty years.

Our main problem now is that the more advanced nations are reluctant to help us to proceed any further with nuclear technology, because they fear that we will then be able to produce our own nuclear weapons.

All the people who work at Atucha I have radiation checks every six months, and those who work in high-risk areas are checked each week. There is nothing to worry about, provided you abide by the safety rules.

Recently, Argentina has begun selling nuclear fuel to Brazil and exporting nuclear technology to other South American countries, such as Colombia, Bolivia, Ecuador and Uruguay. The CNEA is also helping the Peruvian government to build a nuclear power station near Lima.

"Our polo horses are famous all around the world"

Jorge Pittaluga is 27 and runs his family's farm in the heart of Buenos Aires Province. He began playing polo at the age of 10. His ambition is to play in the Palermo Open Cup, the most prestigious tournament in Argentina.

Polo has never been as popular here as soccer or tennis. It was brought to Argentina at the end of the last century by English *estancia* owners. It rapidly became popular with the local farmers and has survived to this day.

In the mid-1920s, the first Argentine polo team went to England, the home of polo, and to the surprise of everyone, won the tournament. Since then, we've never looked back! We play polo in a very aggressive manner, which other nations find difficult to beat. For years, the polo world cup has been won by an Argentine team. Our best polo players own farms where they can practice all year round.

Polo is a good spectator sport – very fast and full of action. We play on a ground 270 meters (295 yards) long and 100 meters (109 yards) wide, with a goal at either end, into which the players try to hit the wooden ball with their sticks. Each game has five or six periods, known as chukkers, of seven minutes, and each team has four players. The winning team is the one which has scored the most goals.

Polo is a dangerous sport. The horses reach high speeds, and if the rider isn't an expert, he can easily fall off – something that happens all the time. I've had a couple of nasty falls where I've fractured my hand and wrist. It's a sport where the player needs a great deal of concentration and strong arms and legs to control the horse.

A good polo horse is fast, strong and not too tall. The best ones are bred from a good mare polo horse and a racing stallion. Our polo horses are famous all around the world, and people come here to buy them. I breed and train horses for sale abroad.

We begin training horses when they are only fifteen days old, and it usually takes a year to get them to the right standard. Horses begin playing in matches at the age of five. We use them for three or four years, then, if they're good, we keep them for breeding.

My ambition is to play in the Palermo Open Cup, the most important tournament in Argentina and famous around the

Polo is a dangerous game, with horses reaching high speeds. Even expert riders often fall off.

world. The first round is played during the spring, with the final at the beginning of December. Only the top six teams in the country take part. To play in the Cup, you've got to be very good and own at least ten pedigreed horses. In polo circles, people say that the horse is at least 60 percent of a good player.

After the Cup, the best people go to Europe or the U.S. to play professionally, earning very good money. In Argentina, we don't have any professional polo players.

Polo is a good spectator sport – very fast and full of action, but not as popular as soccer or tennis.

"350 species of birds and animals"

Alberto Casaroli, 26, has been a warden at the Iguazu National Park for two years. The park is in the northeastern part of Argentina, near the borders of Brazil and Paraguay. Alberto had to take an eighteen-month course to become a warden.

I first came to this park ten years ago. Things have changed a great deal since then, particularly the facilities for visitors. Now there is a luxurious five-star hotel for them – with beautiful views.

The Iguazu National Park was set up in 1937. It has a sub-tropical climate and is 53,000 hectares (132,500 acres) in area. The Iguazu waterfalls are the main attraction. There are 287 waterfalls in the park, the largest one being *La Garganta Del Diablo* (the Devil's Throat) which is more than 100 meters (330 feet) high.

There are 21 parks in Argentina, covering 1 percent of its total area – that's about 27,900 square kilometers (10,730 square miles). And more are being planned. Each park has its own special attraction. The Laguna Blanca (White Lagoon) Park, in the Province of Neuquen, was set up to protect the black-collar swan. The National Park of Pozuelos, near the border with Bolivia in Jujuy Province, was opened in 1979 and contains three of the five known species of flamingoes in the world.

There are three main parts to my job: keeping an eye on the animals, trees and plants; helping scientists with their projects; and public relations – showing people around. At the moment, I'm involved in a project at a local school where the children are being encouraged to take more notice of their natural environment.

There are fourteen other wardens at this park; not enough really for a park this size, especially at the height of the tourist season – from July to October. But we're hoping to get some more help.

Generally speaking, I've found that the typical Argentine visitor isn't very interested in, or concerned about, nature and doesn't really appreciate what can be seen in this park – the 350 species of birds and animals, and the hundreds of different types of trees and tropical plants.

(Right) The Iguazu waterfalls are an imposing sight, especially after it has been raining.

"We eat more meat than any other nation"

Oscar Vilora has been driving a cattle truck for the last twenty-two years. Born and bred in Santa Fé, he has driven all around the country and says he knows every town and village! Oscar works for one of the largest transportation firms in Argentina.

My company transports animals to the national market in Buenos Aires from every part of the country. There they are bought by the *frigorificos* (meat-processing companies) and their meat is either sold for our own consumption or exported.

Our own demand for meat is very high. We Argentines really like meat and I've been told that we eat more meat than any other nation. But meat is an important part of our export business, too. Balancing the two has caused us problems. We have tended to consume too much of our meat production. A few years ago, we killed too many animals. This caused an increase in the price of meat, which meant that our exports of it fell.

After the animals have been sold, we transport them to the *frigorificos* which bought them. I work for one of the largest transportation companies in the country. It owns 100 trucks. A driver is paid a basic wage, plus 17 percent of the total amount earned by his vehicle. So we try to transport as many animals as we can in the least possible time. It's a job with little rest and no fixed hours. We work all hours of the day or night if necessary.

Transporting cattle by road doesn't cause many problems. We stop every

Oscar's firm transports cattle to the market in Buenos Aires, and from there to the frigorificos.

Oscar works for the largest transportation firm in Argentina. It owns 100 trucks, like this one.

couple of hours to check that no animal is lying down, because the others could easily trample it to death. Trains are rarely used now to carry cattle because it's not so easy to keep an eye on them.

In my truck, I can carry 20 calves or 40 old animals. The meat from calves and steers is more valuable than that of the old animals, so we have to take good care of them. Older animals' meat is used to make sausages. When we load and unload the trucks, we give the animals a mild electric shock with a rod connected to a battery. This is better than hitting them with a stick, which leaves marks in the meat.

Our roads have improved greatly during the last ten years. I can remember when we used to bring animals from Corrientes down to Buenos Aires, a distance of 1,000 km (625 miles), and it took four or five days. The roads were in a very bad state and we had to cross the River Parana by ferry, which caused long delays. Now, with a tarmac road and a new bridge over the river, the journey takes only twelve hours. With improvements like these and modern Ford and Mercedes trucks, my job has become much easier, allowing me to move more cattle and so earn more money. There are still poor roads in the south of Argentina, in Patagonia. It can take you more than eight days to travel about 3,000 km (1,875 miles). We transport sheep up from Patagonia to the Buenos Aires markets.

"120 to 150 carcasses an hour"

Rosa Valdes, 45, cuts up meat in a *frigorifico* near Buenos Aires. It is one of the largest in Argentina, employing nearly 700 people. Meat and its by-products are very important to Argentina, forming about 11 percent of its total exports each year.

I've been working at this *frigorifico* for six years. My job is to remove the tendons and fat from the meat, and cut it up according to the customer's wishes. It's a job that is traditionally done by women because of the dexterity needed, although there are some men working with us. I started here as an apprentice, doing odd jobs, and then was taught how to use a knife to cut up an animal's carcass. Now it takes me about six minutes to prepare the meat for packing. Between 120 and 150 carcasses are cut up and packed every hour.

Cutting up the meat is traditionally done by women, because of the dexterity needed.

The frigorifico *where Rosa works is kept very clean – both inside and out.*

Our meat is exported all over the world, but our main customers are West Germany, Switzerland and Italy. West Germany and Italy are big consumers of vacuum-packed meat. This is meat which is not frozen, but sealed in plastic bags with all the air sucked out. It keeps fresh for thirty days after being packed. It's more expensive, but better quality.

Because we are export-oriented, we only use meat from first-class bull calves. The calves are brought here either direct from the many *estancias* in Buenos Aires province or from the cattle market in the capital.

In theory, once a calf has arrived here, it's possible to kill it, cut up the carcass and pack the meat in fifteen minutes! But, in practice, to obtain the best quality, we let the carcass hang for two days in cold storage before cutting it up.

Like all the other *frigorificos* in Argentina, we are visited frequently by the government's meat inspectors, who check the quality of our meat and make sure that the strict hygiene laws are being obeyed. They have the power to shut a *frigorifico* if they find that the laws are being broken.

I work for five and a half days a week – 7 a.m. until 4 p.m. (with one hour for lunch) Mondays to Fridays, and 7 a.m. to 11 a.m. on Saturdays. It's hard work, so I really look forward to my vacations. I get three weeks a year, which I usually take in February, during our summer. My husband and our three children either go to La Rioja to see my relatives, or to one of the vacation camps the meat workers' union owns in Cordoba and Santa Fé.

31

"The first man-made lake in South America"

Dr José Galindez is a retired lawyer. He has been Mayor of Villa Carlos Paz since 1980. On the shores of a lake, the town is a fashionable vacation resort in the center of Argentina. Many Swiss and Germans have emigrated to the town, and still continue to do so.

This town is named after Carlos Paz, who founded it in the 1920s. It is located on the shores of the first man-made lake in the whole of the South American continent. We are 30 km (19 miles) from Cordoba, the largest industrial city in Argentina after the capital.

We have always been a tourist resort for the inhabitants of Cordoba and were only really "discovered" by the rest of the country in the late 1960s. Since then, our population has more than tripled – from 40,000 people to 150,000. Now we have the highest building rate in the whole of Argentina. Recently we have been actively promoting ourselves as an ideal place for business conferences. Most of our restaurants and hotels are now open throughout the year. We have 250 hotels in the town.

Excluding Cordoba, most of our tourists come from Buenos Aires and Santa Fé. People from Brazil and Uruguay also come here for vacations. Possibly because of the similarity of our landscape and climate to those of the European Alps, many Swiss and Germans have emigrated here, and still continue to do so. Our winters are warm and dry and our summers are hot and wet. So this is an excellent place for water sports like sailing, windsurfing and water skiing – all of which can be practiced for ten months of the year.

The original name of this place was Valle de Quizquizalate: an Indian name meaning the place where two rivers meet. Even with all this water around here, we have a shortage of drinking water during the main tourist seasons – December to March, our summer, and July, our winter. Hopefully, the problem will be solved when a new dam is built, which will also provide drinking water for Cordoba.

My term as mayor will end in 1983 at the elections for a civil government. Argentina is a federal republic, which means that the provinces are largely self-governing. They have their own parliament and constitution, although some matters, such as the mail and phone systems, the army and certain industries, are controlled

Villa Carlos Paz. Founded in the 1920s, it is now a popular tourist resort.

by the government and national Parliament in Buenos Aires. Within this political structure, our municipality is able to create laws which will protect the character of Villa Carlos Paz. We now have strict laws about new buildings, especially in the center of the town. We would like to see more new apartments and houses, but we also don't want the town spoiled. While I've been mayor, I think that I've prevented the town from losing its charm.

José's modern bungalow is in a beautiful position, overlooking the lake and the town.

"Argentina is a big producer of wine"

Alejandro Sera owns a small vineyard in Mendoza, the wine capital of Argentina. His family has been producing wine for more than a century, and Alejandro hopes that his son will carry on the tradition. Little of Argentina's wine is exported.

Mendoza has a long history of wine production, and it is now the main grape-growing area in the country. Situated beside the Andes, the soil and climate here are ideal for vines. Winters are cold and dry; our springs are warm; and we have very hot summers, with temperature reaching 38°C (100°F).

My family has been growing vines fo over a century, and I hope that my son and then my grandson will continue the tradition. We have our own vineyards and als buy grapes from other producers as well We bottle and sell the wine under our ow label, and also sell it in bulk to companie in Buenos Aires and Cordoba for them t bottle and sell.

Producing wine is quite a simple proc cess. When the grapes are ready, we pres them to obtain what we call the *most* (grape juice). This is left for a few days i cold cellars to ferment. Then it is filtere and put into wooden barrels for a fev months, before being ready to drink. Th more time the wine spends in barrels, th better it is. The best *mostos* of a year ar kept in oak barrels for several years. The are called "reserve wines" and are

The end of the grape harvest is always celebrate with a party – with lots of wine!

grower's top-quality wine.

You have to keep a careful eye on the temperature and decide how much and what sort of chemicals to add to the *mosto* to get a good wine. How much you add depends on the quality and characteristics of the *mosto* each year.

Variations in the weather give the *mosto* its characteristic flavor, so weather is the main preoccupation of a wine producer. If it hails at the time the grapes are starting to appear (usually around November or December in this region), many will be destroyed, resulting in a poor harvest and low-quality wines. Ideally, we want rain and not too much cold at the start of the growing season and sun, lots of it, during the last couple of months, March and April.

Argentina is a big producer of wine, most of it for our own consumption. Argentines like to have wine with their meat. Our national diet is wine, meat and salad! Generally speaking, we are more preoccupied with quantity rather than quality. That's why we don't have a large export trade in wine.

Salta is the other main wine-producing area in Argentina. It has a climate similar to ours, but drier. Less rain means that it does not produce as much wine as Mendoza, and it has a different taste.

This region totally changes during the grape harvest. People come here from all over the country to pick the grapes. It's a hard job and pickers are paid according to the weight of grapes they gather. We celebrate the end of the harvest with a big party, roasting a whole pig or even a calf over an open fire.

A press being emptied after the mosto *(grape juice) has been extracted.*

"Up to 40 schools a day"

José Balseiro, 33, organizes school visits to the Natural Science Museum in La Plata. Founded in 1877, the museum has a world-famous fossil collection, as well as a library containing 58,000 books. José's wife also works at the museum.

The Paleontology (study of animal fossils) Department is the most important section of this museum. It has a collection of fossils, found on the Pampas and in Patagonia, some of which are one and a half million years old. Most of them were discovered by Florentino Ameghino, one of the world's first paleontologists. He lived from 1854 to 1911, and was a director of this museum starting in 1902.

From studying fossils, Ameghino put forward some theories on the origin and evolution of mammals, especially man. These caused a lot of arguments among scientists of his day. Ameghino said that all the mammals of the world, including man, had their origins in Argentina and other parts of South America. His views weren't accepted by his fellow scientists but in recent decades they have been taken very seriously.

Another scientist whose theories on the evolution of species caused a lot of arguments was the British naturalist Charles Darwin. Between 1832 and 1835, he sailed around the South American continent in the *Beagle*, visiting Brazil, Uruguay

The museum's entrance is guarded by statues of tigers that lived on the Pampas 10,000 years ago.

Argentina, Peru and Chile. One of the places he visited in this country was Punta Alta, on the coast near Bahia Blanca. There he discovered fossils of giant armadillos — as big as rhinoceroses! We have the remains of one of these fossils in the museum.

Today, scientists from many countries visit this museum because our fossil collection is one of the best in the world. The general public, too, enjoys coming here. In 1983, we had 500,000 visitors. There is no entrance fee for school children and students, but adults are charged a nominal amount. On Mondays, everyone can come in free of charge.

All museums have two important functions — to preserve the past, and to educate people about it. I work on the educational side and help to organize school tours around the museum, as well as making arrangements for scientists who come here to do some research. My busiest time of the year is in the spring, from September to November, when up to forty schools a day visit us.

Scientists come from all over the world to see the fossils in the Paleontology Department.

"Tango was born in Buenos Aires"

Isabel Gil is 30 years old and a tango interpreter in a club in old Buenos Aires, an area popular with both tourists and locals. She originally trained to be an actress but has been singing for a living for twelve years.

You may think that the tango is typical of the whole of Argentina, but that's not really true. The tango was born in Buenos Aires and I still think that it's the only place where you can see it performed properly. The tango is a mixture of styles and influences brought to Argentina by the immigrants who came to live here from Spain, Italy and Africa.

The place where I work is typical of the many clubs and restaurants in this part of the city. People come here just to listen to the tango and to watch the dancers. The club is situated in San Thelmo, one of the old-fashioned parts of the capital. My customers often tell me that it reminds them of Paris, with its narrow streets, old buildings and late-night cafés and bars. I think it's one of the nicest districts of Buenos Aires.

People who perform the tango are always called tango interpreters, and we take the tango very seriously. It's not like popular dancing in other parts of the world. The tango dance is like a three-minute play, in which the singer develops a close relationship with the dancers. To perform and to appreciate the tango, you really need to be at least 30 years old.

The club where Isabel performs is situated in the old part of the city of Buenos Aires.

Young people simply have not had enough experience of life to perform it properly.

In the old days, the tango was performed in nearly every bar and club in Buenos Aires, but this has all changed. The tango used to be a genuine means of expression, particularly for poorer people. Nowadays, it's often more of a spectacle, put on especially for the tourists.

The most famous Argentine tango interpreter was Carlos Gardel. He died tragically in an airplane accident in the 1930s. Since then, he has become something of a national hero. Many people still go to visit his tomb and leave flowers. Today, Asto Piazzola is our most famous

Today, the tango is usually performed for the benefit of tourists.

tango interpreter and composer. He has created a new style for the tango, which the younger performers prefer, but which has been rejected by lovers of the traditional style.

We tango interpreters are very superstitious. Before I go on stage I always cross myself and pray that our performance will be successful. Some tango interpreters wear lucky amulets or always wear the same tie. I'm always nervous before a performance, but once I get out on stage, all my worries disappear.

"Business is not what it used to be"

Ferdinando Martin is the skipper of a boat on the River Parana's delta, a tourist region near Buenos Aires. He has been working on the river since he was 10, when he used to help his father run his boat.

I began working for this company in 1949 when tourists first started coming to this area. We pick people up at the village of Tigre, about 40 km (25 miles) from the center of Buenos Aires, and take them around the River Parana's delta. It's a beautiful area, full of small channels with an enormous variety of flowers and trees along their banks. During the summer, it's very hot and humid; and in winter it's very mild.

In this area, there are many weekend homes, restaurants and hotels, some of

Ferdinando's boat was built forty years ago in Tigre, but it is still in excellent condition.

Many of the large houses on the Parana's banks have been converted into private clubs.

them very old with beautiful architecture. At the beginning of this century, this used to be a very exclusive "playground" for the rich people of Buenos Aires. When they moved away, many of their large houses were turned into private clubs.

People still come here from the capital and its suburbs, but we also get visitors from the interior and many from abroad, especially Brazil, Germany and Switzerland. Most of them come in the summer, when it's almost impossible to get through all the small motorboats in the channels without an accident.

This is not just a tourist area: many people live and work here, too. There used to be large orange and lemon plantations, but people now prefer to grow poplar and willow trees because they're less of a financial risk. When they're ten years old, the trees are sold for their wood.

During the winter, we act as supply vessels for the inhabitants, delivering their mail and carrying goods. Boats go around the delta every week to sell meat, bread and groceries — floating stores!

This company owns twelve boats, all of the same type and all made of wood. They were built in Tigre forty years ago and are still in excellent condition. Business is not what it used to be. Gasoline and spare parts are very expensive now, and fewer and fewer people are coming here. During the summer, we carry about 130,000 passengers each month; ten years ago it was ten times that number. But so long as people keep on coming here and continue to live here, we'll carry on.

"The best farming land in the world"

Santiago Lara owns a 1,000-hectare (2,500-acre) farm near Bragado, in the heart of Buenos Aires Province. Farming is undergoing a major transformation in the province with many cattle breeders turning to growing crops, especially grain.

I've always been a cattle breeder, but I'm soon going to start growing crops, like many other farmers in the province. A cattle farmer can get hold of money very quickly, merely by selling some animals. But he is greatly affected by the international price of meat and by the government's policies. Because meat is an important part of the national diet, its price is manipulated by the government for its own ends. Lowering the price of meat is popular with the people, but can have disastrous consequences for farmers.

A few years ago, meat prices were kept at a very low level. As a result farmers killed many of their stock because they couldn't afford to feed them. We still haven't recovered from this, and it's going to take a few more years for us to get our stock of cattle back to the right level.

Using the price of meat for political ends has forced many farmers to give up raising cattle in favor of growing crops. With crops, you only get an income once a year – after the harvest. But you aren't affected so much by price fluctuations and by government policies. Also, using the latest techniques, it's almost impossible to lose a crop.

Buenos Aires Province has some of the best farming land in the world, and an ideal climate for both cattle and crops. Millions of years ago, this area was an enormous bay which was gradually filled up with sediments brought down by rivers from the north and east. In time, the sands, clay and alluvium were covered by a thick layer of dust, blown here by the wind. This has turned into a dark, very fertile soil, providing good pasture for fattening up calves before they are sold in the markets in Buenos Aires.

In the north, the Provinces of Entre Rios and Corrientes don't have such a good climate as ours and poorer soils. Consequently, farmers send their animals to the southern part of Cordoba Province or to Santa Fé Province for fattening up.

The western part of Patagonia, in the south of Argentina, is another important

Cattle being sprayed with chemicals to keep them free of harmful parasites.

cattle-breeding area. The rest of that province is used for rearing sheep.

Like most of the cattle in this province, mine produce good-quality meat, most of which is exported. They're very delicate creatures which have to be innoculated against disease and kept free of parasites. They fatten easily, but we have to be careful not to over-graze the land when we are feeding them, making sure that we rotate the pastures so that the grass has a chance to grow again.

Cattle will always be raised in this province, but grain is probably going to become more important.

About 200,000 animals are sold every month at the cattle market in Buenos Aires.

"Peron ... a prophet ... a visionary"

Luis Manzano, 27, is a doctor in Rosario, in Santa Fé Province. He is an active member of the Justicialista Party, which was created by Juan and Evita Peron in the 1940s.

The Justicialista Party was born in 1946 when General Juan Domingo Peron came to power. With his wife, Evita, he created a political movement which was popular with the poor. He helped them with new laws, free education, and many social and economic reforms.

In doing so, he threatened the power of the traditionally dominant upper classes, who supported the *coup d'état* which overthrew him in 1955. Peron went into exile in Spain. He returned here in 1973

Political parties began preparing for the October elections in the summer of 1983 with ads like this one.

Argentina's Parliament, closed since 1976, was re-opened in December 1983.

and was elected President, only to die a few months later. His second wife, Isabel, replaced him.

Argentina has been independent of Spanish rule for almost 170 years. During this time, there have been many political upheavals with both civil and military governments trying to run the country. The last civil government – Isabel Peron's – was overthrown by the military in 1976. After making many errors, the military were forced to call elections. These took place at the end of October 1983, and were won by the Radical Party. It formed a government in December.

Our party has three million members and is divided into a male branch, a female branch, and a trade union branch. Its leaders and policies are chosen at a national congress, attended by party representatives from all the provinces.

I've been a Justicialista since I was a little boy. My family supported the party right from the start. When I was young, I heard my father constantly talking about

its plans.

But I didn't become a member because of him. I became interested in politics when I was at school, and joined the party while at the university. As a doctor, I cannot ignore the suffering that I see around me, and I firmly believe that my party can solve many of the problems Argentina has.

The party is stronger in the provinces than in the areas around Buenos Aires, where one-third of the population lives. Rosario has always been a Justicialista town.

For people like me, Peron was and still is a prophet, a visionary, a father-figure. He once said that, by the end of the century, Argentina will either be a strong, united country or a weak one, dominated by more powerful and advanced nations. My party thinks that a lot has still to be done if we are not to remain an underdog in world affairs.

45

"A farmer who can grow cotton, can grow anything"

Ana Solis is 23. She lives in Santiago del Estero, in the province of the same name. She is completing a five-year course in agriculture by spending a year with INTA, a national organization which gives farmers advice on the best ways to use their land.

Cotton has been grown in Argentina for at least 400 years. When the Spaniards arrived here in the sixteenth century, they found that the Indians bartered cotton for goods.

Growing cotton has always been a complicated process, involving a lot of people. Even today, there is little mechanization: sowing, harvesting and controlling the weeds is largely done by hand. Preparation of the soil starts in July; the seeds are sown in September; and the crop is harvested in March. In Argentina there is a saying that a farmer who can grow cotton, can grow anything.

The amount of cotton grown is affected by the economic policies of the government. There have been times when its cultivation has been encouraged, and then we have had 700,000 hectares (1,750,000 acres) of it growing; in other years, less than half that amount of land has been used. This province usually produces about 12 percent of the total production of Argentina. At present, we are producing only 2 percent because of unfavorable economic policies.

In 1982, INTA began a campaign to try to improve the situation. It has been helped by the provincial government, which has provided loans to cotton farmers. We hope that this province can return to its previous levels of production by improving efficiency and the quality of the crop, and not solely by increasing the amount of land with cotton on it.

In past years, cotton production has been affected by cheaper synthetic fibers. But cotton now seems to be regaining the markets it lost. Most of the cotton grown in Argentina is not for export. Our own textile industry needs about 130,000 tons of cotton a year to cope with demand. Now that we are producing better quality fibers, our exports are increasing.

In this province, as in all the other main cotton-growing provinces (El Chaco, Corrientes and Formosa), cotton has been grown by many farming families for generations. Growing cotton alone on your land

is not good for the soil. So INTA is encouraging farmers to practice crop rotation to improve the soil.

INTA (the National Institute for Agricultural Technology) was set up in 1956. It now has offices and laboratories all around the country to give farmers advice.

Recently-picked cotton being unloaded at a mill in Santiago del Estero Province. This province produces 12 percent of Argentina's cotton.

At the mill, the cotton is processed into large bales, ready for transporting to textile factories.

"80 percent of our grain goes to Russia"

Rumualdo Diaz owns a small farm and is also a part-time cook and a worker at an agricultural cooperative. He lives in Lima, a quiet little town in the Pampas, in an area which grows a lot of grain.

I own a small farm and also work occasionally as a cook for the big parties of the important families of Lima. My speciality is roasting a complete animal – skin and all! It's difficult to do and takes around fourteen hours.

This area is famous for producing grain – especially corn and wheat – and sunflower seeds and soy beans. There are many agricultural cooperatives around here, like the one I work part-time at, where farmers have gotten together and built silos to store the grain in after it has been harvested. The grain is kept in the silos until it is sold by an agent to foreign countries. Then it is taken to the port in trucks, especially designed to unload the grain quickly at the terminal.

Until recently, the truck owners didn't like carrying our crops because there wasn't much money or work in it for them. But now, with grain production increasing and with more storage silos being built to store it in safely, they can be guaranteed work for ten months of the year.

Most of our grain is taken to the port of Buenos Aires, some 160 km (100 miles) away, for exporting: 80 percent of it goes

Silos for storing grain are becoming a common sight on the Pampas.

The town of Lima, in Buenos Aires Province, is situated in the heart of the flat Pampas.

to Russia. This situation has both advantages and disadvantages. Russia pays us a good price, but we have lost our other markets, making us too dependent on one buyer. Over the years, the government has built up a good fleet of merchant ships to transport the grain abroad.

Our biggest competitor in the grain markets is the U.S. Its government helps its grain producers with good credit facilities, something that doesn't happen here. Consequently, we cannot expand our production because we lack the money to buy more seeds and land.

The main grain producer in Argentina is Buenos Aires Province, where the soil is so good that farmers don't use fertilizers except for growing wheat. The province

used to be important for raising cattle, but technological advances in agriculture and the discovery of hardy and more productive seeds have made grain farming less risky and more profitable. The southern part of the Province of Cordoba and the Province of Santa Fé also produce grain, which is exported through the port of Santa Fé, on the River Parana.

Patagonia used to be an important grain producer, but sheep rearing is now its main agricultural activity. This hasn't affected the overall pattern of grain production, because more farmers are now using their land for growing crops.

49

"Bariloche is famous for its chocolate"

Juan Alonso works in a chocolate factory in San Carlos de Bariloche, in the south of Argentina. Situated on the shores of Lake Nahuel Huapi, the city is the country's main winter resort.

The chocolate industry started in Bariloche forty years ago when an Italian immigrant realized that a nourishing hot drink would be ideal here during the cold winters. So, he went back to Europe and brought back a recipe from Switzerland and began to produce chocolate. It was a tremendous success. Now Bariloche is famous throughout Argentina for its chocolate.

Located in the south of the country, on the edges of the Andes Mountains, this region doesn't produce many of the ingredients for the manufacture of chocolate. Milk and sugar have to be brought from Buenos Aires and cocoa is imported from Brazil. But this has not been an obstacle to the industry's growth.

The chocolate is made from sugar, cocoa and cocoa butter. These are all mixed for four days in a special machine. In low-quality chocolate, the cocoa butter (which is very expensive) is replaced by glycerine and animal and vegetable oils. The less cocoa butter you use, the more unpleasant the flavor is.

Bariloche, on the shores of Lake Nahuel

The chocolate factory where Juan works. It was the first one to be opened in Bariloche.

Huapi, was founded in the seventeenth century by a Jesuit priest who came across the Andes from Chile. Destroyed many times by the Indians, it became a real town in the late nineteenth century. Now it's the main winter resort of Argentina, well-equipped with an airport and many hotels and restaurants.

Situated so close to Chile, we have many visitors from there. During the summer, we also cross the mountains to swim in the Pacific Ocean, which is much closer to us than the Atlantic.

Full of lakes and rivers, this region is ideal for fishing. International and national championships are held here each year. During the season, you can catch trout weighing up to 12 kg (26 lb).

In the summer, you can go to Port Panuelos and take a trip around the lake, seeing the beautiful myrtle forests and many waterfalls. The water is so clear that you can see the bottom of the lake, more than 20 meters (66 feet) below you.

On the shores of Lake Nahuel Huapi, Bariloche becomes crowded in winter with skiers.

"Gambling must be in our blood"

Italo Colluccini began his working life as a trainee croupier in a casino. Today he is the director of the Casino Nacional in Mar del Plata. With 170 roulette tables, his casino is one of the largest in the world.

Mar del Plata is the main tourist resort for Argentina. It is 400 km (250 miles) from the capital and is famous for its long sandy beaches. The resident population here is about 385,000 but in the summer season, which in Argentina is between November and Easter, it is flooded by more than a million visitors.

People of all classes spend their vacations here. For the rich, there are the luxury hotels and apartments. Poorer people stay in the "family hotels" or in cheap boarding houses.

Argentines love gambling. I think it must be in our blood. Our casino, together with two others in the city, is the main attraction here for many people. At the height of the season we have upwards of 15,000 people in here every night. During the Holy Week of 1983 (the first week in April) we had to close the doors of the casino one night when there were 35,000 people inside.

Except for one in Catamarca, all casinos in Argentina are owned and run by the state. Casinos can be found in most of the main cities around the country, from Iguazu in the north down to Comodoro

Roulette is the main attraction for people at the casino where Italo is a croupier.

The seafront of Mar del Plata. The casino is the building on the right.

Rivadavia in the south.

The main attraction for our clients is the roulette table. No one knows for certain who invented the game, but tradition has it that it was devised by a priest in the seventeenth century. The story goes that there was a king who loved to collect different games. But he always found that after a while he got bored with playing them. The king heard of a priest who had the same hobby and asked him to invent a game which would never bore him.

After a year, the priest returned with the game of roulette. The king was delighted but again got bored with the game; this time because he was fed up with losing. He called the priest in again and asked him to find a system for winning at roulette. The years went by and the priest, unable to find a way, eventually committed suicide. Which I suppose goes to show that you can never win at roulette!

For the tourists who don't come here to gamble, the area has lots to offer. Travel firms take people inland to the *estancias* at Chapadmala and Ojo de Agua where they can watch rodeos and folk-dancing.

"I would like to see fewer foreign series on TV"

Silvia Rolandi is a newscaster who works for the local television station in San Miguel de Tucuman, where she was born and brought up. She is looking forward to the day when there will be less government control of broadcasting.

My busiest time of day is between 10 a.m. and midday, when I interview people for the evening news program which I present with a male colleague. The program is in color, so you have to be careful about the make-up and the clothes you wear. Color television only started in this country in 1978 when we had to update our equipment for color transmissions of the World Cup soccer matches to other nations.

In Buenos Aires, there are five television stations that produce virtually all the national programs. They sell them to the one hundred or so local television stations for broadcasting in their own regions. Local stations also produce their own programs.

Since 1973, almost all the television stations have been in the hands of the state. The station I work for is owned by the University of Tucuman and the provincial government. In some places, like Salta and Santiago del Estero, the local stations are in private hands.

I think that all television stations should be run by businessmen to minimize any government manipulation of the news.

Silvia often gets recognized in the streets and does not mind stopping for a chat.

During the Malvinas War (the Argentines call the Falkland Islands the "Islas Malvinas") in 1982, the truth about what was happening was kept from the people until the very end. Now that we have elected a civilian government, we hope that all broadcasting stations will be leased to private enterprise. This is something that's been long awaited.

In the future, I'm hoping to produce a program for women. I don't think that women participate enough in this country's development. It's not our fault: we're still looked down upon. But I hope I can begin to change attitudes. During the Malvinas War, I wanted to go to the islands to do a program on what was going on, but I wasn't allowed to — because I was a woman!

I would like to see fewer foreign series on our television, especially the ones from the U.S. We need to produce more of our own programs that reflect our way of life and give us a real sense of identity.

A couple of years ago, I had the chance to work for a television station in Buenos Aires, but I didn't like the competitiveness and loneliness of that big city, even though it has more opportunities to further your career and ambitions.

I much prefer living in Tucuman. This region is famous for its flowers, especially roses. Most of Argentina's sugar also comes from this province.

A lot of sugarcane is grown around San Miguel de Tucuman, where Silvia lives and works.

"Like all Argentine families, we eat a lot of meat"

Marcelo Roa is 12 years old and lives in Buenos Aires. He is in the seventh grade, his last year at elementary school. After five years at secondary school, Marcelo wants to become a car mechanic.

I go to a state-run elementary school which was built over a hundred years ago. My classes start at 12:30 p.m. and end at 5 p.m., Mondays to Fridays. We have two quarter-of-an-hour breaks, during which the senior pupils, like myself, make sure that the younger ones behave themselves!

The school is in a densely populated part of Buenos Aires, so there is a lot of traffic in the surrounding streets. At the end of school, the senior pupils are in charge of stopping the traffic so that everyone can cross the street safely.

I enjoy going to school because I have many friends in my class. Also, we don't do much work in class and get little homework! I have lessons in nine subjects: math, Spanish, science, history, geography, geometry, art, music, and handi-crafts – plus sports, of course.

You don't have a uniform at elementary school, just a white coat to wear over your clothes. But I'll have to wear a uniform at secondary school – gray trousers, white shirt, blue tie and jacket, and black shoes. Very neat!

Every pupil at a state elementary school is given a glass of milk and a piece of bread

Senior pupils stop the traffic to allow children to cross the streets after school has finished.

and butter during one of the breaks. I usually drink the milk but leave the bread!

After school, I usually go off to an empty parking lot with a group of friends for a game of soccer, or to a café which has pool tables and pin-ball machines. By law, minors are only allowed to stay in these places until 9 p.m.

On most Saturdays, I go to the movies with a gang of friends. Afterwards, we go back to one of our homes and have a party. On Sundays, my family goes out to a recreation club on the outskirts of the city which we belong to. My brothers and sisters and I play in the swimming pool while my father prepares an *asado* (barbecue). Like all Argentine families, we eat a lot of meat, and my father's *asados* are delicious! If we don't go to the club, I go off to Palermo, a district of Buenos Aires that's full of parks where people go for all sorts of sports.

On Sundays, Marcelo often plays soccer in a park in the Palermo district of Buenos Aires.

Facts

Capital city: Buenos Aires.

Principal language: Spanish, with many local variations. English is used throughout the country as the second language. In Patagonia there is a large population of Welsh-descended settlers who still speak Welsh. A language called *Lunfardo*, made up of words from many languages, is spoken in the capital by some people.

Currency: 100 centavos = 1 peso; 24 pesos = U.S.$1 (spring 1984).

Religion: Over 90% of the population is Roman Catholic, which is the official religion of the country. But freedom of worship is written into the constitution and is observed in practice. Religious faiths or sects can be banned if they are considered to be damaging to public order, morality or national security. Religion is particularly strong in rural areas.

Population: 27,862,771 (1980) – an increase of 19% since 1970. Argentina is comparatively under-populated: just over seven and a half times the size of Great Britain, it has just over half its population; over a third the size of the U.S., Argentina has about one-eighth of its population. 79% of the population live in urban areas – 9.7 million people in Buenos Aires and its suburbs. People have been moving from the countryside to the cities, so large parts of the interior are sparsely populated. The population is predominantly white and of European origin. Many Europeans emigrated to Argentina at the end of the last century. There is a large British community. Recently, many Bolivians, Uruguayans, Paraguayans and Chileans have settled in the country. In the far north, at least half the people are *mestizos* (mixed Spanish and Indian), although they comprise less than 2% of the total population. In the highlands of the northwest and in southern Patagonia, there are still a few pure-blooded Indians. Blacks and mulattos (people of mixed black and white parentage) have disappeared.

Climate: Varies between sub-tropical in the north to sub-arctic in Patagonia. The central area has a temperate climate. The climate is influenced by oceans and the high mountains in the west. Much of Argentina is arid or semi-arid.

Government: Argentina is a federal republic with a constitution which is based largely on that of the U.S. Politically, the country is divided into one Federal District (Buenos Aires), 22 Provinces, and one National Territory (Tierra del Fuego). The latter, by a decree in 1957, includes the South Atlantic dependencies of South Georgia, the South Shetlands, the Argentine Antarctic Sector and the Islas Malvinas (Falkland Islands). Following a military coup in 1976, Argentina was governed by a junta, made up of the three commanders of the armed forces, until December 1983. Then a civilian government was formed by the Radical Party, following its victory at the elections in October 1983 – the first in nine years. Argentina's Parliament which had been shut since the coup, was re-opened. The 22 provinces have a large amount of self-government. Each is administered by an elected governor.

Housing: The influx of rural workers to the cities has created housing problems. Slums, called *villas de miserias*, have developed. Housing conditions, in general, are of a higher standard in Argentina than in other South American countries, but adequate housing for workers and for lower-income groups is still a problem.

Education: Education is free from pre-school (kindergarten) to university level. There are also private fee-paying schools. Education is compulsory for the seven grades of elementary school (from 6 to 13 years old). Secondary schooling (from 14 to 17+) is optional. There are 29 government-run universities and 23 privately-run ones.

Agriculture: Out of a total land area of 2,766,889 square kilometers (1,068,302 square miles), 65% is used for agricultural purposes: 13% of this is for

Glossary

growing crops, 52% is pasture land, and 22% is covered with forest. Of the total crop area, 25% is taken up by wheat and 15% by corn. Other important crops are sorghum, grapes, potatoes, sunflower seed, soy beans, sugar and yerba. Argentina is the world's largest source of tannin, which is used to turn hides into leather. A high proportion of farmland is held by large ranches devoted to cattle raising. The vast Pampas of central Argentina, an area as large as France, provides excellent conditions for cattle grazing throughout the year. In 1980, there were 60 million cattle and 35 million sheep. Argentina is virtually self-sufficient in food. The average Argentine eats more meat than anyone else in the world. Agriculture accounts for 85% of the goods exported.

Industry: Most of it is concentrated in and around Buenos Aires – 70% of imports come in through its port. Meat-packing and processing are very important. Also important are flour-milling, sugar refining and wine. In recent years, textiles, plastics and engineering industries have expanded. Argentina is rich in natural resources, particularly coal, gold, silver and copper, all of which are being developed. The country hopes to become a petroleum and gas exporter. In 1977, the main imports were machinery, chemicals, iron and steel, oil, and ships. The main exports were cereals, meat, oils and fats, animal feeding stuffs, fruit and vegetables, machinery and wool. The top three destinations for exports were the Netherlands, U.S. and Brazil. The top three sources of imports were the U.S., West Germany and Brazil.

The Media: There are 350 daily newspapers, 760 periodicals, and 960 weekly newspapers and magazines. The daily newspapers published in Buenos Aires are available around the whole country. All the major provincial cities have their own newspapers. There are 65 TV stations, 4 of which are in Buenos Aires. About 3.8 million TV sets are in use.

amulet A piece of jewelery worn as a lucky charm.

coup d'état A sudden, violent overthrow of a government, usually by the armed forces.

crop rotation Growing different crops, in a planned sequence, on the same piece of land so as to maintain or increase its fertility.

estancia A large cattle ranch.

frigorifico A meat-processing factory.

gaucho A cowboy of the Pampas, usually of mixed Spanish and Indian descent.

maté A small metal bowl, out of which yerba is drunk. Sometimes used for the drink itself.

pampas The extensive, flat grass plains of central Argentina. The western part is largely barren. The eastern part, which has a higher rainfall, is covered with tall, coarse grass, known as pampas grass. The pampas are similar to the prairies of North America, the steppes of the U.S.S.R. and the veld of South Africa.

rodeo An outdoor show where people display their riding skills, such as riding bareback or on untamed stallions.

roulette A gambling game in which a ball is dropped on to a spinning wheel, divided into 37 colored and numbered slots. Players bet on the number and color the ball will fall into.

silo A large cylindrical building in which grain is stored until needed.

tarmac A hard surface of crushed stones, bound together with tar, which is used on roads and airport runways.

Acknowledgements

The photograph on page 15 was supplied by the Alan Hutchison Library (Moser).

Index

Agriculture 10–11, 15, 16, 20–21, 42–3, 46–7, 48–9, 58
Ameghino, Florentino 36
Andes mountains 8, 16
Apostoles 10
Army 13
Arts and culture
    folk-dancing and song 6–7, 17, 21, 38–9, 53
    museums 36–7

Bariloche 50–51
Buenos Aires 9, 12, 13, 28, 29, 38, 39, 43, 54, 55, 56, 57
Buenos Aires Province 8, 20, 21, 24, 42, 48, 49

Cattle farming 8, 20, 28, 42–3
Chocolate industry 50–51
Climate 58
    in the Andes mountains 16
    in Buenos Aires 12, 40
    in central Argentina 32
    in Mendoza 34, 35
    in northeast Argentina 26
    in Patagonia 14
Cotton industry 50–51
Crop farming 42, 48–9
Currency 58

Darwin, Charles 36

Education 26, 37, 56–7, 58
Elections of 1983   45, 55
Entertainment 57
Estancias 20, 21, 31
Exports
    of arms 13
    of grain 48, 49
    of meat 28, 30, 31, 43
    of nuclear technology 23

Falklands (Malvinas) War 55
Festivals 17
Fishing 51
Food 21, 28, 35, 48, 57
Forestry 41
Fossils 36, 37
Frigorificos 8, 28, 30–31
Fruit industry 15

Gaiman 14
Gambling 52–3
Gardel, Carlos 39
Gauchos 20–21
Government, The 58
    and control of media 54, 55
    and cotton industry 46
    and meat industry 31, 42

Housing 17, 58

Iguazu waterfalls 26, 27
Incas 7
Indians 14, 16–17, 20
Industry 59
INTA (National Institute for Agricultural Technology) 46, 47

Justicialista Party 44–5

Language 15, 58
Lima 48, 49
Local government 32, 33

Malvinas (Falklands) War 55
Mar del Plata 52, 53
Maury, Mr 8
Media 59
Mendoza 34, 35
Merchant fleet 49
Military service 12–13
Military government 45
Minerals 8, 23
Monasteries 18

National Parks 26
NEA (National Commission for Atomic Energy) 22, 23
Nuclear Power 22–3

Pampas 20, 48
Parana River 40–41
Patagonia 9, 14, 20, 29, 42, 49
Peron, Evita 44
Peron, General Juan Domingo 44, 45
Peron, Isabel 45
Piazzola, Asto 39
Politics 44–5

Polo 24–5
Population 58

Railroads 8–9
Religion 58
    Catholicism 18–19
    Indian religion 17
Roads 20, 29
Rodeos 21, 53
Rosario 44, 45

Salta 6–7, 8, 18, 19, 35
San Martin, General 12, 13
Spanish influence 7, 18, 20
Sugarcane 55

Tango interpreters 38–9
Television 54–5
Tourism 17, 32–3, 39, 40–41, 51, 52, 53
Transportation 28–9
Tucuman 54, 55

Villa Carlos Paz 32–3

Welsh immigrants 14
Wildlife 26
Wine industry 34–5
Women, status of 53
Wool industry 15

Yerba plantations 10–11